You're Dumber in the Summer

And Over 100 Other Things
No One Ever Told You

by Jim Aylward

illustrated by
Jane Chambless-Rigie

Holt, Rinehart and Winston / *New York*

10 9 8 7 6 5 4 3 2 1
Library of Congress Cataloging in Publication Data

Aylward, Jim.   You're dumber in the summer.

Summary: A collection of more than 100
little-known facts about such topics as food,
the brain, and animals.
1. Curiosities and wonders—Juvenile
literature. [1. Curiosities and wonders]
I. Chambless-Rigie, Jane. II. Title.
AG243.A9   031'.02   79–1147   ISBN 0–03–043551–X

Contents

To Nell Aylward, my mother,
who told me a lot, but *never* told me
any of these things.   J.A.

The pictures are for Mitchell.   J.C.

Introduction

There are times in your life when your mother will tell you things you should know. Sometimes your father will tell you things. Once in a while Grandma will tell you what's what. When you have a question you can always go to Uncle Fred. At school Miss Regish will explain certain things in detail that you may not even want to know. All through life good people will take you aside and tell you things, sometimes when you don't even ask. But there are some things *no one ever tells you,* and over 100 of them are in the pages of this book.

Animal Antics
Birds, Bees, Bugs, and Bears

Your rabbit can see behind himself.

Bees can't see red, but they can see ultraviolet light.

Fish and snakes can't blink.

A jellyfish can't see at all.

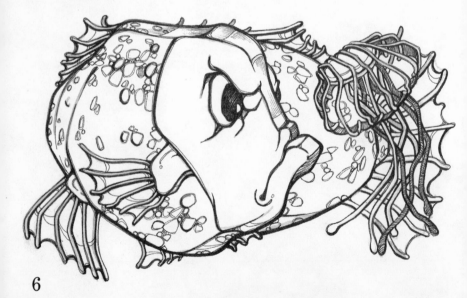

If you thought Big Bird was big, there was once a bigger bird. About four hundred years ago there were reports in New Zealand of a huge bird called the moa. At nine feet tall, weighing five hundred pounds, it never got off the ground. Today, of course, there ain't no moa.

7

Your friendly neighborhood squirrel climbs down a tree just the way he goes up . . . headfirst. Check it out.

The giant anteater of South America has a giant appetite. He can put away thirty thousand termites a day.

The world's largest animal was the pre-historic eighty-thousand-pound stegosaurus. It had two brains, one in the head and another in the tail. The stereo stegosaurus?

A hog runs
at a top speed
of eleven miles
per hour.
Pig power.

The sloth eats so slowly, by the time he gets one meal done it's time for another. That's slow.

A rabbit will never perspire. Rabbits are always nice to be near.

All fish are born without scales.

If you take care of a cow by herself she'll give more milk than a cow in a group.

Your goldfish can get a headache from you tapping on the tank.

A wise old owl isn't. Owls have low IQ's.

A dolphin has at least the intelligence of a seven-year-old child. Some scientists think it's much higher.

Your cat can't count, but any cat can tell what time it is. Lunchtime especially.

Biologists are saying they can cross a goose with a swan now to make a swoose. Of course, nobody needs a swoose. There's no use for a swoose.

Food
Things to Know about that Stuff You Eat Twelve Times a Day

America's favorite food is the hamburger. It accounts for up to 30 percent of all nationally sold meat today. It's possible to eat a different kind of burger every day for a whole year without repeating.

NO ANCHOVIES

There are only three grams of protein in two slices of baloney. That's baloney. It's also the truth.

Americans are going bananas. They're our favorite fruit. Everybody in this country eats nine pounds of bananas a year.

Apple pie is not our favorite dessert. Strawberry shortcake is the winner. Banana or lemon cream pie is in second place. Apple comes in third. Grapenut pudding isn't even listed.

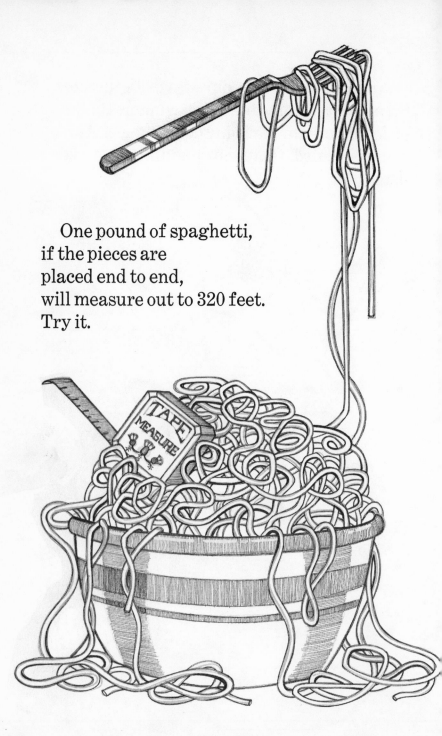

One pound of spaghetti,
if the pieces are
placed end to end,
will measure out to 320 feet.
Try it.

The average mother in this country cooks 57,000 meals during her lifetime.

When Grandma uses saffron in cooking supper, she's actually sprinkling in crocus blossoms. That's what saffron is.

Famous Names
Including Yours

One out of every four boys in the U.S.A. today is named George, Charles, James, William, or John. That's just about every Tom, Dick, and Harry.

Adolf Hitler had sinus trouble and only four of his own teeth.

The ten most popular last names in America today are Smith, Johnson, Williams, Brown, Jones, Miller, Davis, Martin, Anderson, and Wilson.

The third most popular name in the Manhattan telephone directory?
Wrong. It's Wong.

A school in California had to have trophies for a spelling bee redone. They misspelled the winners' names.

The Facts of Life
The Truth about Noses, Toeses, and Much More

The first word said on the moon was "Houston."

Every United States president with a beard was a Republican.

The average parent spends $2.66 a week at the supermarket on things children ask for.

In the late 1500's tobacco was considered by many doctors to be a wonder herb. They used it to cure toothache, falling fingernails, halitosis (bad breath), lockjaw, and cancer.

Your nose just keeps on growing all through your life.

Your hearing is the sharpest just before sunup. I SAY YOUR HEARING IS . . . Never mind.

A forty-watt fluorescent tube is as bright as a regular one-hundred-watt bulb.

When you rub your eyes and see a flash of light with both eyes closed, that's called a phosphene.

Recently a group of researchers counted the number of troubles there are in the world. They came up with a grand total of 2,653.

In the summer on a hot day, the tempera-
ture inside a parked car is about 160 degrees.

If you have to do some heavy thinking today, lie down. You think best when you stretch out on a couch or bed.

Today only 22 percent of all the drivers on the highways ever use their seat belts.

The word "posh" dates back to late-Victorian times when the English traveled by sea to India. To avoid the glare of the sun in the Red Sea, travelers paid extra for the cabins that would be on the shady side during the hottest part of the day. They traveled Port Out, Starboard Home. Posh!

Your Aunt Bertha's face-lift is supposed to last five to ten years. After that, doctors say, she may need a minilift. Or a maxi mask.

If your great-granddaddy had an earache, he corrected it by wrapping onion skins around his toe.

Those plastic holders for coffee cups without handles are called zarfs.

Brains
Things about Your Thinker

Your brain can store away ten new bits of information every second.

When some of the world's most gifted people were youngsters they found "brainwork" difficult. Albert Einstein caused considerable anxiety because he was slow to learn to talk. Galileo was refused a doctor's degree. Charles Darwin was told by his father that he would become a disgrace to himself and his family. Thomas Edison was at the bottom of his class. James Watt, who invented the steam engine, was considered a dull child. Emile Zola, the famous writer, got a zero as a student of literature.

The average human brain, weighing three pounds, occupying one-tenth of a cubic foot, and needing only twenty-five watts of electricity to run it, can store between 10 billion and 100 billion items of information.

The good old summertime is when you're at your mental bottom. If they give you a test in August you may not pass it. Give you the same test in April and you'll handle it easily. You're dumber in the summer.

Health
Information on Keeping Fit

If you burn your finger, stick it in your ice cream. Ice cream is good stuff for burns. Then bathe the burn in lukewarm or cold tea and you won't get a blister. If you already have a burn blister, the tea will make it go away quickly.

The average breakfast cereal has 11 percent protein and a handful of vitamins and minerals. Your dog's dry meal has 20 percent protein, 4.4 percent fiber, and so many vitamins and minerals it fills fourteen lines of print. A can of dog food contains more nutrition than your favorite fast-food-restaurant hamburger.

Watching television for hours may be hard on your eyes and/or your intelligence, but it can also seriously damage your teeth. Dr. Robert L. Cook of New York City says it's the leaning of the hands against the lower part of the face that does it. The pressure of the hands can easily cause children's teeth to move around.

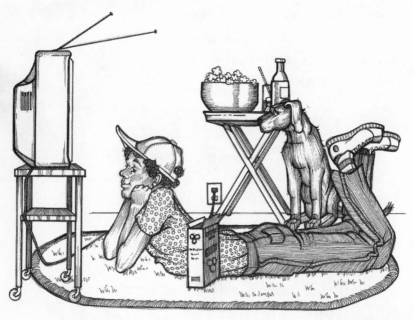

Large amounts of acid may be as harmful to your teeth as large amounts of sugar. A researcher at the University of Iowa says so. He tells us that when large amounts of lemon, grapefruit, and orange and their juice are consumed, the acid attacks tooth enamel and can erode it. Pickles can do it too.

The reason you can't sleep some nights is the fear of not sleeping. But by just lying there thinking good thoughts you'll get as much rest as if you had slept all night.

The best way to help sore, aching muscles is to put up for the night in a sleeping bag. It keeps you warmer than a blanket.

If you're an average person you may lose your temper six times a week.

An element called potassium is necessary for health. It helps the central nervous system transmit electric currents essential for your brain, muscles, heart, and nerves. You get potassium from bananas, oranges, and vegetables.

Cold weather does not cause colds. Doctors say the reason more of us have colds in the winter is because we're inside more where we may be overheated and breathing dry, stale air.

An hour of tennis burns up five hundred calories. Bicycling for an hour burns up five hundred, too. If you swim, however, you use six hundred eighty-five calories an hour.

Stung by a jellyfish? Get out the meat tenderizer fast. That's the most soothing remedy for the sting of a jellyfish.

Kids suffer the same stomach ailments adults do. Even ulcers.

You tend to catch colds when you're feeling guilty about something you've done.

Europe now has a double-headed tooth-brush. It lets you clean top and bottom teeth at the same time. It's all the rage for big-mouths.

Homemade chicken soup is the best medicine when you have a cold. The *American Heart Journal* says it has the same animal and plant tissues as found in the human body, and it's perfect for replacing body fluids. So, your mother *is* right.

If you want to have more vigor so you can play harder, take a nap today. A daily half-hour nap will make you stronger.

No single exercise is better for you than walking.

A half hour of exercise just three times a week can noticeably slow down aging. You're worried about that already?

Hay fever is an allergic disease that is not caused by hay and does not involve a fever.

Some medical people say it's perfectly okay for a ten-year-old to sleep with a teddy bear. When you get to be twenty, however, check with your doctor.

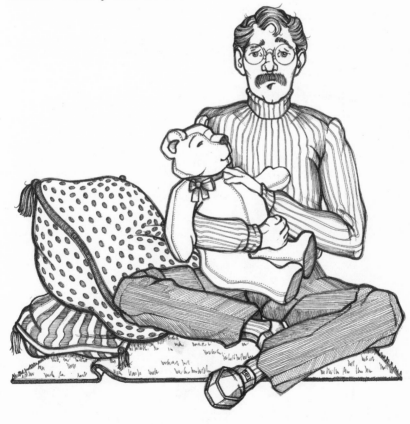

Around the World
Notes on Anything
from Anywhere

The Great Wall of China is so long it would reach more than halfway across the U.S.A.

In Mexico City the air is so polluted that breathing it is the same as smoking a couple of packs of cigarettes a day.

In South America your standard diction-
ary is called a *mata-burros*. *Mata* means kill
and *burros* are, of course, jackasses. Carry-
ing a mata-burros under your arm will kill
your image as a jackass.

Some 10,000 to 12,000 years ago it was
possible to walk between North America and
Asia. You crossed from Alaska to Siberia on
a natural land bridge that later disappeared
beneath the rising waters of the Bering
Strait.

British ice cream isn't made from cream at all. It's made from pig fat.

Russian dancers and singers must retire at the age of forty.

The English have a little game they call Noughts and Crosses. We call it Tic-Tac-Toe.

Weight
Facts on Fat, Lessons on Lean

Eighty-five percent of all chubby children turn out to be chubby grownups.

If you think you're overweight, grasp the flesh just above your waist between your thumb and the tip of your forefinger. If you pinch more than an inch it's a cinch you're a fatty.

When you hear somebody say that overweight is caused by glands, don't believe it. Doctors say only a very small percentage of overweighters have a glandular problem. It's not the glands. It's the mouth.

Fifty million Americans are overweight.

Crazy Facts
Strange, Weird, but Positively True

Your toenails have gold in them. But nobody knows why.

When you have a peanut-butter sandwich you're actually eating pea butter. A peanut is not a nut. A peanut is a pea.

The car on the back of that ten-dollar bill is a Hupmobile.

A tattoo is a commitment for life. There is no way one can be removed without a trace.

Americans talk more on the telephone than any other people in the world.

The merry-go-round was dreamed up in Davenport, Iowa, back in 1871.

If you haven't seen a rainbow lately it could be due to pollution. Rainbows and dirty air don't seem to mix well.

One hour of tap dancing provides as much exercise as two hours of rigorous calisthenics.

If you're hot in the summer you'll cool off faster with a warm drink. A cool drink only cools the area around your mouth.

Researchers at the University of Washington have invented a hearing aid that's worn around your middle, not on your ears. They say the skin of the stomach can be trained to detect speech if it's transformed into electrical impulses. The researchers say the hearing aid's only disadvantage is it tickles. (What? You say you think you hear a hamburger?)

Bee stings and lightning
kill more people
than snake bites.
By the way, Hawaii and
Alaska don't have snakes.

ALASKA OR BUST!

During World War Two, auto tires made of wood were tested. They worked nicely on smooth roads but they chipped if they hit a pothole. If you changed a tire you got splinters.

Your two ears are different. In fact, no two ears are ever alike.

That old wild man of the West, Wild Bill Hickock, curled and set his hair with perfumed wax. Nobody ever mentioned it. At least not to his face or his curly hair.

You tend to hear an earthquake before you feel the shaking.

More than 25 billion toys have been given away in boxes of Cracker Jack.

Almost half the people in offices at the top of skyscrapers get motion sick on very windy days. Those buildings are designed to sway as much as three feet.

If you were to grow as fast as a baby whale grows, you'd be about sixty-five feet tall by the age of two.

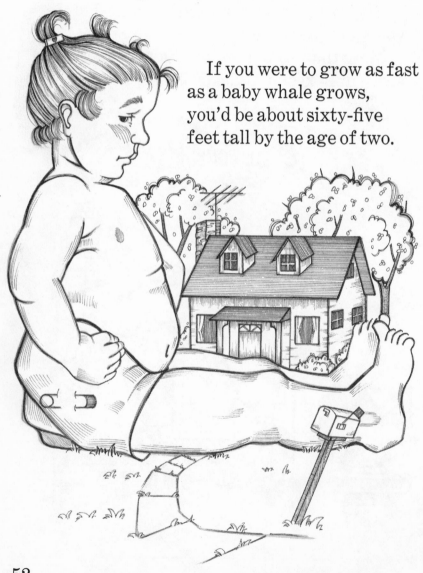

Scientists at Purdue University claim to be producing electricity from spinach. They attached an ordinary automobile battery to a plate coated with chlorophyl from spinach. They say when the sun shines the spinach produces electricity. Maybe if you eat your spinach you'll glow in the dark.

Your birthday is not yours alone. You share it with about 9 million others in the world.

If they turned off the air conditioning at the Houston Astrodome, the entrance of humid air would be so great, it would rain inside the stadium.

It pays to watch your punctuation. In November of 1962 a little hyphen was left out of a set of instructions directed at a Venus space rocket. The rocket self-destructed.

One of the earliest cures for arthritis is from the world of gypsies: To lie down on hard-packed earth and let a brown bear walk up and down on your back. (It really does work if you can bear it.)

If you want your family to live longer than anybody else around, get them to move to Lincoln, Nebraska. Today, for some reason, people in the U.S.A. live the longest in that area.

Miscellaneous
That Means a Bunch of Stuff that Doesn't Go Together

You cannot determine whether a person is male or female just by analyzing his or her handwriting.

If you want people to look up to you as a leader just keep talking. If you talk more than others, no matter what it is you say, your friends will think you're a giant.

The leading career choice of seniors in top-rated high schools today is medicine. Science and communications come next.

If you're an extrovert you like red, orange, or yellow. If you're introverted you prefer blue, green, or purple.

Turning a light bulb on and off will shorten its life.

The family car uses a cup of gas every six minutes while the motor idles.

Girls like boys with thin legs and a moderately tapered V look. That's what they like, but they don't find many because most boys don't look like that.

If there's a bump on your nose don't worry about it. Face researchers say bumpy noses mean you're ambitious, full of energy, and very generous. Your nose is generous, anyway.

English teachers give better marks to students who use big words in their essays, even if the essays are poorly written.

If you check your Italian you'll find that the word *spaghetti* actually means "little strings."

If you want to get more respect, walk tall. If you slouch, people will think less of you. Walk tall and they'll think of you as a success.

If you're an only child, you score higher in verbal ability and professional status than children with brothers and sisters. Famous "only children" include Hans Christian Andersen, Franklin D. Roosevelt, Robert Louis Stevenson, and Queen Victoria. You're also a high scorer if you're the oldest of several children.

If you just broke somebody's window with a baseball, you're not alone. About 4,000 windows are smashed every year that way.

If you see a flying saucer, call 800 348-4057. It's the International UFO Registry.

Mosquitos like men more than women and adults more than kids.

You're the shy, retiring type? Four out of ten Americans are.

People who have been to college do better economically than people who only went to high school. They're less likely to be unemployed and are more likely to have higher average incomes.

If a baseball game takes about two and a half hours, only eight minutes of that time is action time.

Psychologists say if you have an unhappy
childhood you may, surprisingly, become a
happy adult. Adults who make the biggest
successes in life and are happiest in their
work seem to have had the most difficult
times as children.

About the Author

Jim Aylward is host of one of America's most popular early morning radio programs, "Jim Aylward in the Morning," on WRFM in New York City. He also writes a syndicated newspaper column, "Jim Aylward's Journal," for United Feature Syndicate. His popular feature "Things No One Ever Tells You" started on radio, was extended to newspapers across the country (including the *Indianapolis Star*, *Albany Times-Union*, and the *Bergen Record*), and now appears as a book for young readers.

About the Illustrator

Jane Chambless-Rigie is a free-lance illustrator who lives on Long Island, New York.